ANGELIQUE CHAPMAN
RICO GRADY
HOW FAR WOULD YOU GO TO HELP A STRANGER?
Mile 19
"MILE 19"
BUFFALO 8 AND HOWARD CLAY FILMS IN ASSOCIATION WITH MARK FEATURES
EXECUTIVE PRODUCED BY: MATTHEW HELDERMAN LUKE TAYLOR RABESHIA CLAY ANDREA PAUL HOWARD CLAY JR.
MUSIC BY: JULIAN JOHNSON DIRECTOR OF PHOTOGRAPHY: CHRIS ORR EDITED BY: NICOLE BAER PRODUCTION DESIGNER: ANDREA PAUL
STARRING: ANGELIQUE CHAPMAN RICO GRADY VIVIAN GIL ASSIA LAU'REN EUANTON DOTSON JEROME JOHNSON
PRODUCED BY: RABESHIA CLAY WRITTEN AND DIRECTED BY: HOWARD CLAY JR.
HOWARD CLAY FILMS
buffalo 8
A BONDIT COMPANY
WWW.HOWARDCLAYFILMS.COM

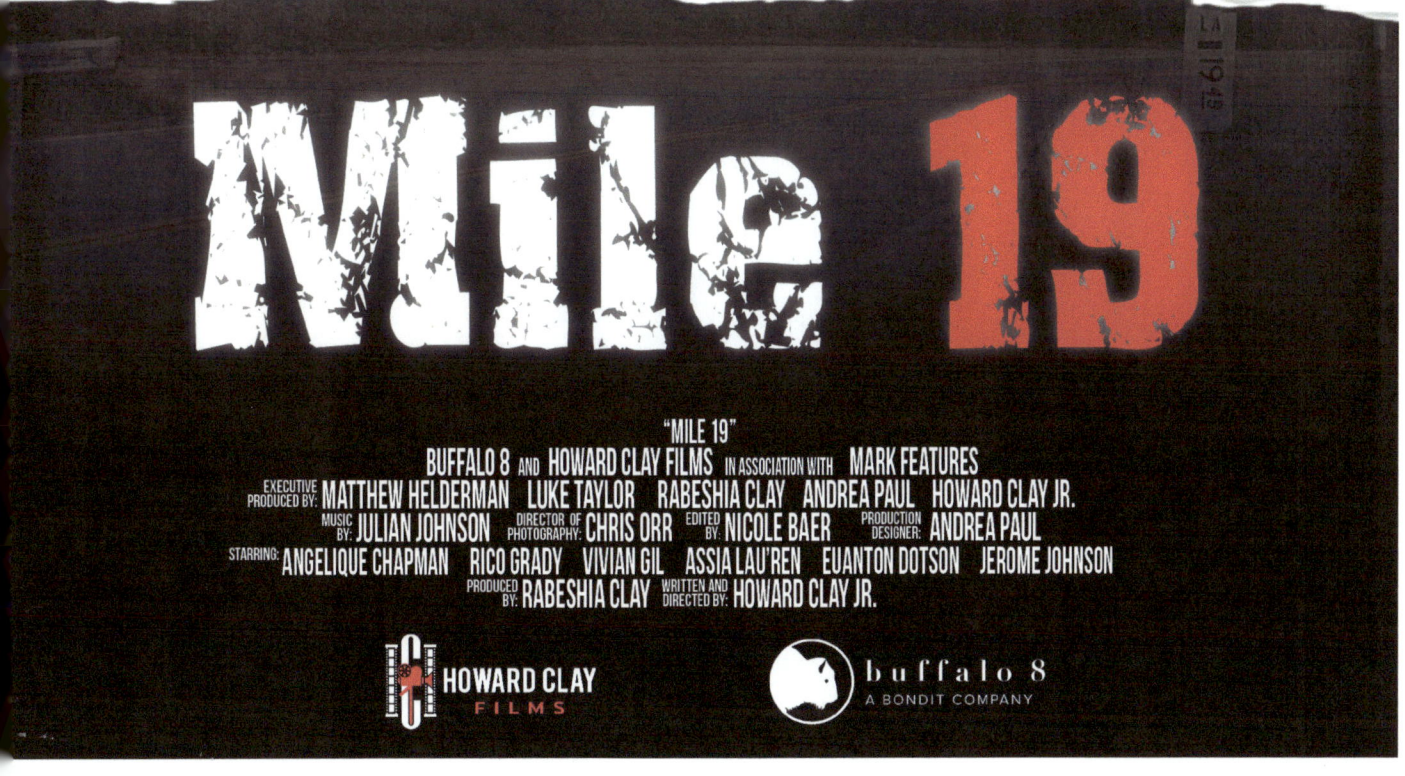

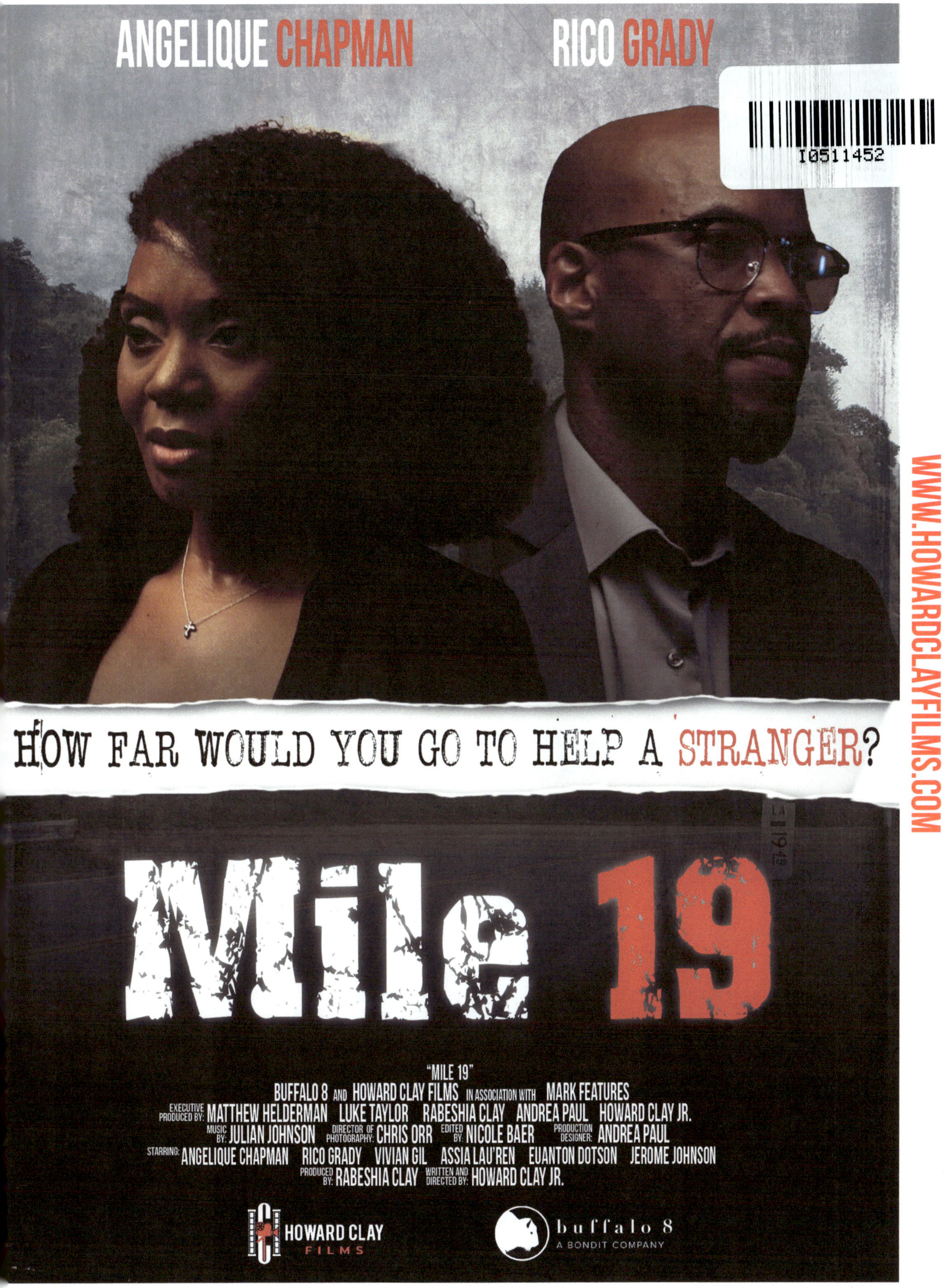

Section 1

16
Cover Interview
Jesse Collins
talks about his crazy, but successful path to being a boss!

Pure Heat Community Festival
Pg: 11
First Year, First Impression
Pg. 12
The In - Between Time
Pg. 14

Section 2

24
Young B.O.S.S.
Lady Key
She speaks about building an empire, from the ground up.

Young B.O.S.S. : Lady Key
Pg. 24
Keep'n It 100
Pg. 25
The Institutional Racism Behind Reaching Proficient
Pg. 26

Section 3

40
Entrepreneur to watch for 2016

DJ FADELF
Pg. 42
Jerome Pearson
Pg. 52
Sherry Reed
Pg. 48

11
Monica

Pure Heat Community Festival

Cover Interview: Jesse Collins
Pg. 16
Sign Your Own Checks!
Pg. 22

30
J.C. Banks

The one WOMAN who will revolutionize the art of Weddings!

#BuildAsWeClimb
Pg. 28
WebWed
Pg. 30
Fvmly
Pg. 32
B.O.S.S. HBCU
Pg. 34

"Women Of Small Businesses" Profile Highlight
Pg. 44
Women Winning In The Federal Government Contracting Space
Pg. 46
Artisans From South Africa Excelling in American Markets
Pg. 50

B.O.S.S.
Magazine
Substance In Every Issue

STAFF

Board of Directors

Martin T. Shepherd
Esq. EQT Corporation

Dr. Adrienne Booth Johnson
CEO - Infinity Global Connections

Aisha Felder
*Principal Marketer
of Red Shoe Marketing Group*

Tiffany Harden-Evens
Esq.

Linda Clay
Chaplain

Founder/Publisher
Howard Clay Jr.

Co-Founder/Editor-in-Chief
Andrea Paul

Art Director
Emmanuel Johnson

Editorial/Digital Content Manager
Cierra McClurkin

Marketing and Advertising Manager
Desha Elliott

Media Relations Manager
LaTresa "Tree" Cunningham

Promotions Director
Jeffrey "Royce" Clay

Contributing Writers:
Vincent Cunningham
Natyana Robertson
Angel Amos
Adam Sanders
Dr. Gillian Berry
Ebbie Parsons
James "Jay" Bailey
Marcia Robinson
Desha "DrDesha" Elliott

South Region Advisor
Gloria Ishman

North Region Advisor
Pamela Thomas

Cincinnati Regional Ambassador
Myeeah Scott

Fort Valley State University Rep
Natyana Robertson

Contributing Editors
An Howard

Photography
Tristan Ervin
Anthony Tyus
Larry Person

Interns
Ciara Green
Lizandro Falu
John Kelly

B.O.S.S Magazine

Editor's Note

Andrea Paul
Editor-In-Chief
@Drea_Elizabeth

Andrea Paul is available for speaking engagements, clinics/ seminars, as well as appearances for organizations, corporate and school events.

For Booking
drea@boss-emag.com

Find a way or make one.

Even though I went to Clark Atlanta University for one semester, their motto has stood out to me since Fall 2010. Whether you are an entrepreneur or intrapreneur (fill in the following blanks to fit your preference) the CAU motto should speak to you as well.

When a person decides to go the entrepreneurship route, most likely, their initial thoughts were to solve a problem in a specific way. To that person, the old ways of doing things seemed obsolete, so they set out to change the game. For intrapreneurs, the same rules apply, but instead of venturing out on their own to build things from the ground, up, they decide to work for a company and utilize their skills to change processes within that company. Whether that means they are looking to get a promotion to a higher position, or even if they find a way to save a department money.

_____-preneurs make a way out of no way. They either find a lane, or they make their own. I know you have come across Facebook profiles, Periscope broadcasts, or even spam mail that introduces you to the world of "coaching" and how you can make 6 figures if you start your own Instagram business… The list goes on. In the back of your mind, you probably see those and think "Coaching? Yeah, no." But, guess what these coaches have figured out?

People have pain and the services the business owners address that pain.

Find a lane or make one.

As a _____ -preneur, you must sell your solution to other's issues. That's how you get clients/ customers. Regardless of which route you take in which ever field you decide, you target a need and fill the void. Do it better than the next person or do it differently.

No matter what, _____-preneur or not- you should always find a way to be your own success story at the end of the day.

Find a way or make one.
-        Drea

Publisher's Desk

Last week, I volunteered at the National Black College Alumni 30th anniversary Hall of Fame Program in downtown Atlanta. It was an amazing, yet exhausting experience. The entire weekend consisted of panels, workshops and ceremonies for our current HBCU students an alumni. Kings and Queens competed for scholarships on Saturday and Chairman of the weekend was one of our former covers, Will Packer!

Next to all the pretty dresses and nice suits, there is one image that sticks out in my mind from the event. A young girl, no older than 8 or 9 years old, was walking into the program on Saturday with her mom. All of the college students were lined up in support of their schools' queen and it was a little chaotic. The girl stood there patiently with her mother waiting for their chance to go into the ballroom. She looked eager and slightly excited, but nothing really too special.

And then it happened.

Last year's Queen NBCA Hall of Fame Elisa Thomas, walked by and the little girl's face lit up with JOY. Not just a regular "oh, wow," but pure, unadulterated JOY. It was like she was staring at an angel or the president or something! She looked back anxiously at her mother, who wasn't really paying attention, and then quickly turned back around to stare at the queen walking by. As she watched the queen's every step, I could see the little girl's every emotion. She looked inspired, motivated, and thrilled, all in one. That moment was truly was the highlight of her night.

This is what we should strive for when it comes to motivating our children towards education and leadership. We should find out what gives them that hope, that gleam in their eye, that excitement in their face that will help them be a better student, person, and above all, human being. Too many times we put on programs and events to celebrate ourselves or to make someone else look good, but we have to go back to being an inspiration for the ones watching. For the youth, who need someone to look up to, someone to believe in, something to inspire them. We need more programs like the NBCA Hall of Fame Weekend. We need more programs that cater to the youth and not our own, adult agenda in order to capture the pure joy of believing that anything is possible and that dreams do come true. That's what we need.

So, as your week begins, or ends, think of how you can change the world. What events can you host or organize that will inspire and make the youth believe again?

It is our responsibility as leaders and trailblazers to go above and beyond our own interest and reach the interest and the hearts of the youth.

~   Howard

Pure Heat Community Festival

Atlanta, Georgia

Atlanta, Georgia is currently ranked the top city for newly diagnosed cases of HIV/AIDS in America.

Unfortunately, with there being a lack of knowledge and awareness about the disease, this issue has now since become an epidemic. However, in light of this matter, there are an assortment of organizations, clubs, and events that seek to promote awareness and education regarding the disease. The Annual "Pure Heat Community Festival" (Atlanta, Georgia) is one of those entities that has placed HIV/AIDS Awareness at the forefront.

The "Pure Heat Community Festival" served as a collection of social events that were centered around the actual Festival that happened on Sunday, September 6th. The events ran from Thursday, September 3rd – Monday, September 7th (Labor Day). The events had a variety of celebrities present, including Monica (singer), LaLa Anthony (*LaLa's Full Court Life*), Tiny (*T.I. & Tiny*), and Honored Guest, Kelly Price (singer), who received a Humanitarian Award on behalf of the festival.

In the era of HIV/AIDS being an epidemic, it's a necessity for there to be an abundance of knowledge regarding this illness, because knowledge and education are powerful. Hopefully, with efforts like "Pure Heat Community Festival," the term "HIV/AIDS" will become a distant memory due to the communities increased knowledge of the nature and progression of the virus.

For more details and about the "Pure Heat Community Festival", please check out their website http://pureheatcommunityfestival.com.

Pray, Proclaim, Prosper,
Vincent Cunningham
MindPHulAdvice.com
Instagram & Twitter:
@MindPHul_Advice

First Year First Impression

By: Natyana Robertson

Fort Valley State University '19

Party over here, whoo whoo! Party over there, whoo whoo! Wait. I have an exam tomorrow. It's time to be responsible and make some important decisions. I paid to come to school to get an education, so the parties can wait. I came to Fort Valley State University not knowing anyone, but knowing I belonged at the school. That may sound weird, but there's a feeling I get when I'm on campus, like I *belong* here. Now, first things first, forget the myths and everything you heard about being a freshman in college. Hopefully, by sharing my experiences, all your doubt and fear will go away.

Fast forward to Thursday, move-in day! This was a bittersweet day for me because I was happy to be going off to college, but sad to be leaving my best friend-- my mom. My parents and brother helped me move in and thank God my room is on the first floor! It was crazy that day. There was stuff and people *everywhere*. After meeting my roommates and getting my room set up, it was time for Freshmen Ceremony. This was where we said bye to our parents and I met my friend Mike. Now, not everyone you meet or talk to you is going to be a friend. You have to watch what information you disclose to those you don't know. Mike became my friend because we have the same major, interests, goals, and we encourage each other. I was hanging out with Mike and my roommates until I found my other two friends that I hang out with now. That seems to happen. If you don't know anyone at your school, you may tend to hang with your roommates since you live with them. Going through freshman weekend you will start to see people's true colors since you are the only class on campus at this time. Parents aren't around anymore, so everyone will be doing what they want, now that the weekend is over and the freshmen have a feel for the campus. When the Upperclassmen finally move in, that is not the time to start acting like you have no home-training. Upperclassmen are people going to school just like you, so there is no need to lose yourself over them. In my opinion, college is supposed to be a place to grow. You can't grow if you're focused on others and not your education. It's like what people told me before I came to college, stay true to yourself and remember where you came from. Now that the weekend is over and the freshmen got a feel for the campus, it's time for classes to start.

Monday morning came and reality set in for a lot of people who stayed up late the night before. I know I went to sleep, even with all the excitement going on because I had an 8 o'clock class that morning. I tried to schedule all my

Be your Own Success Story

Photo by Angel Amos

"College life is what you make it."

classes in the morning so my day will end early. Every day, I finish classes at 2pm which gives me time to go study, do homework, or even take a nap!

Stay on top of your work! I didn't know professors slipped in pop quizzes, but when I failed one for my English class, I started looking over my notes everyday. Even when you don't have a class, look over your notes. If you need additional help, don't be afraid to ask for it. I am getting tutored in math by a student organization on campus. Don't wait until your grades are suffering to get help… it will pay off in the long run.

A big tip: *If you're bored on campus, it's not because there is nothing to do, it's because you are choosing not to do anything.* At my school they post flyers all the time for organizations you can join or for events happening on campus. It's up to you to get involved on campus. I'm involved with the campus choir and campus ministries. These things keep me busy with meetings and rehearsals. Now, if you're getting involved on campus, don't overwhelm yourself to the point you're so tired from meetings you can't stay awake to finish a project for class. Your schoolwork comes first; after that, *then* you can prioritize with extra activities.

College life is what you make it and I'm having a great time at my school. Remember, stay focused and stay on the right path. Partying is okay every now and then, but that's not what you paid your money to go to school for. I hope by sharing some of my experiences, you will be excited about your own first college impression!

The In-Between

Navigating between high school and college

By: Angel Amos

"Who would've thought?"

The question I've asked myself constantly over the past few weeks. An honor roll student, honor graduate, multiple scholarship recipient, currently not in any college, at all? I have no idea how to respond when people ask, "How is college going?" or "Why are you still here? I thought you were going away for college.."

Who would've thought that *I* wouldn't be in college right after high school? Don't get me wrong, I am not trying to boast, but in high school, I knew (along with everyone else) that I had everything together when it came to going to college. I knew where I wanted to go, what I wanted to do, and I had received the scholarships to make it happen, but there was one thing I didn't have-- control of my stubbornness. By the time senior year of high school began, I had my standardized tests done, college essays, and recommendation letters all ready to submit. When it was time, I had applied to only two colleges out-of-state colleges. The first, a PWI, I applied to because I absolutely loved it and it was my top choice school. The other, an HBCU, I only applied to because I just wanted to have at least one more option in case my number 1 didnt work out. Everyone, starting with my parents, kept telling me to apply to more schools just to keep my options open, but there was nothing inside of me that said I could possibly end up going anywhere but where I wanted to go. I was even offered better scholarships from other schools than what mine offered but still… I wasn't interested in anything else. I was accepted and received scholarships from both schools and that, to me, said it was *meant* to be.

I was *meant* to go away for college, so when summer vacation began, I was on my way to tour those two colleges. I visited my first choice, the PWI, first. I loved the campus, the people, the weather, the beach, the sidewalks, stop signs, the grass, and everything else that went along with the University. However, when I spoke to financial aid, they let me know in the nicest way possible that I didn't have nearly enough money in my account to attend their super expensive, out-of-state school. So me, as confused as ever, let it go in one ear and out the other because there was just no way I wouldn't be going to this school in the Fall. Afterwards, I went to tour the other school, and being the HBCU that it was, I felt like I had never left home. I wasn't fond of the campus, but the school itself was a good school. I just still could not see myself at that school. However, I had received more than enough financial aid to attend this school, but, I was still stuck on my first choice. I had to figure out a way to get an extra $18,000 to start college in the Fall. Obviously, that didn't happen and by this time I had wasted so much time "figuring it out," it was already the end of July and most colleges were starting orientation and classes in just a couple of weeks. So, I ended up making the decision that I would stay in-state to save money and then just transfer once I got more scholarship money. It seemed so simple because the only thing I had to do is get accepted to an in-state school and start, right? Wrong. Instead, I was denied to my State school because I submitted the application too late. Or at least, that's what I was told.

So, now what? I had missed every opportunity to start college 'on time' and it was all my fault. What would I be doing during the 'in-between time?'

Well, I decided to focus on something I enjoy, and that is photography. I got a job working for a photography company and I've been doing a lot of freelance and other photo shoots. I also got certified to be a practicing nursing aide in two states since it would look good for nursing school applications. After all, that was the plan before financial aid and my poor planning took control. But, since my plans were delayed, altered, throwed, deferred, whatever-- I am able to learn so much and prepare a lot more. Someone once told me that my 'in-between time' is like my extended break from school. I think that's a good way to look at it because while I'm on break, I am picking up on the whole 'adulting' thing. I am learning about the world, people, and other things that will be essential for me once I start college. I've learned that college isn't a race, it's more about how vital those 2 or 4 years are for setting you up for the future. I finally figured out that I'd rather not rush to college unprepared and that it is perfectly okay to start late, be ready, and finish strong. So, when I'm not beating myself up about how much of a failure I am for not starting college in the Fall like the rest of the students from my high school who had credentials no better than me, I am learning, photographing, and overall, spending my extended break 'getting ready'.

Anyone who is deciding to go to college should definitely consider if they are mentally ready beforehand. If that means taking some 'in-between time' to learn about life and yourself before just diving in, I say, "go for it!" No one should rush to college because if you aren't ready, it will be very easy for you to fail and that is not what college is for. My 'in-between time' and all that I've learned so far is what's going to make me a high achieving college student. Whether I start college in the Spring, Fall of next year, or two years from now, I know I'll be ready because I spent the time learning and preparing for what's to come.

Photo by Angel Amos

"So now what? What would I be doing during the in-between time?"

Jesse Collins
Cover Interview

Jesse Collins, the go-to producer for the BET Awards, BET Hip Hop Awards, UNCF An Evening of Stars, BET Honors, Soul Train Awards, and executive producer of the mega-hit TV series Real Husbands of Hollywood starring Kevin Hart, has made a name for himself in the world of television and entrepreneurship. Read about this NAACP Image Award winner's untraditional path to becoming the B.O.S.S. of his own production company and his life!

B.O.S.S.: After high school, what motivated you to get into the entertainment industry? Was becoming a DJ your first choice?

Jesse: No, I wanted to be Arsenio Hall! I wanted to have my own talk show or I wanted to work with Arsenio Hall. "Arsenio Hall" was the long term goal. Then, there were plenty of people along the way who were in line with that (goal) and mentored me along the way. When I graduated from high school, I really didn't know what I wanted to do. Right away, I got a job at a radio station as an intern. I was giving out t-shirts, working in the research department, and doing whatever else I could just to be around the building. My cousin, Melvin Lindsey, was a successful DJ in Washington and he started the "Quiet Storm" with Cathy Hughes (Founder of Radio One and TV One). The idea of being on the radio seemed like a great thing and the closest thing to "being Arsenio Hall" that I could do at the time, so I sought advice from him all of the time. Melvin told me, "you just have to go, you have to find a way in and work from there…"

B.O.S.S.: How important was mentorship in your growth as a professional?

Jesse: I think mentors have been everything for me. I didn't go to college-- it just wasn't in the cards for me. There were always people who would advise me and help me. I was someone who could sit and listen to people who had done what I was trying to do. I was fortunate that a lot of doors were not closed for me, meaning, I was blessed to have so many individuals spend their time with me and give me that extra 5 minutes. I was never afraid to ask questions. Whatever I was doing, I was not afraid to learn more.

B.O.S.S.: Did you approach these mentors or did they see something in you?

Jesse: I feel like I was always the aggressor! (laughs) When I worked at the station, I would call one of the DJs, Donnie Simpson (original host of BET's first video program, Video Soul), all the time! Usually, it was for NO reason… just to ask him about anything I could come up with. Donnie was the type that would at least answer the phone 1 out of 3 times. He would answer questions about life, radio, developing a voice, or whatever. The questions were ridiculous but, he would always give an answer and was always supportive.

Section 1 - Cover Interview

"If you quit, failure is absolutely certain. If you keep trying, then winning is a possibility."

Cover & Interview Photography: Drexina A. Nelson, Photographer | Styling: Arike Rice
Producer: Staci R. Collins Jackson for The Collins Jackson Agency

Cover Interview - Jesse Collins

Photo Courtesy of BET Networks

B.O.S.S.: You have an unconventional way you reached your success. What would you credit as your biggest break to get to where you are today?

Along with this, there was a series of events that set me up to have the confidence I have to do what I do today. That is what I think is so pivotal to success; the preparation starts way before the opportunity or the moment.

B.O.S.S.: You said you thought you could offer more...where did your confidence come from in that moment?

Jesse: As we were talking and as I was asking questions about what he wanted and needed the show to be, I realized that I knew some things that brought more to the table than just writing. I had some insight on what the show for the 20th anniversary of BET should be—what needed to be celebrated and what some of the essential elements that had to be a part of the show should be. That's when the light bulb went off for both of us and realized I can do more.

B.O.S.S.: You have a certain level of "grind" when it comes to your work. What would you say is the amount of grind or effort needed to reach a level of success?

Jesse: I think it's non-stop. There isn't a lot of sleep and it requires a lot of focus. If you look at everyone who is great at what they do—doctor, lawyer, business owner, athlete, mechanic, rapper, anyone—the common thread between them all is the amount of effort they put in to being great at that one thing. Money comes when you are great at something! (Laughs) I once watched a documentary with Quincy Jones where he spoke about how important it is to focus on something and be the best at it. The money and the accolades come fairly easily once you've become the best. The trick is that it takes a lifetime to become the best at something; a lot of work, effort, pain, and struggle. But, if you focus on being the best, everything else will be achieved. It works itself out. If someone comes to me for a job and the first thing they ask is about the pay rate, that tells me they are not focused on being the best, nor on trying to further their skill set. They are just thinking about getting paid- which is fine, but then that method of reinforcement gets maxed out you will reach a ceiling. If, on the other hand, you walk in and say, "What are you guys doing? What can I do to help? Here is what I can offer. This is what I want to achieve," I can tell they want to aspire to something GREATER than the cash. You have to find that fine line.

B.O.S.S.: Through your career, you've found a lot of success. I know it was a bumpy road along the way. What motivated you to keep going despite the obstacles?

Jesse: Growing up, I witnessed a lot of things. Feast to famine, money in and money out. My parents would grind constantly, in success and in failure because they didn't really have a choice. What option do you have? Quitting should never be an option, maybe changing direction, maybe doing something else, but quitting should never be an option. If you quit, failure is absolutely certain. If you keep trying, then winning is a possibility. Very successful people have always told me

> "If someone comes to me for a job and the first thing they ask is about the pay rate, that tells me they are not focused on being the best, nor on trying to further their skill set."

that. If you quit you have NO shot. I'd always rather have a shot. Some people have always been there for me in my "down times" and have stepped up to help me. Like, when I lost my job in radio and didn't know what to do and I was running out of unemployment checks. one of my best friends sat me down with Robert Townsend who asked me about what I was doing next. I replied that I was not leaving LA, but was literally, a week from poverty. He said, "What do you think of writing?" Then, he gave me a script, told me to punch it up, and see if I could put jokes in it and I did that. From there, he put me on the show Parenthood. The first month there, I was just showing up to The Writer's Room and writing. I was working for free and I knew not to bring up pay because I wasn't supposed to be there. Afterwards, the studio found out I was working, and they kicked me out. The head writer/producer told me to sit tight because they would figure something out and that was it. That was a tough time for me, but the work paid off. People who believed in me were very beneficial and I was just focused on being the best I could be. So, when unforeseen things happen, people will have noticed that you gave your best and you worked hard, so they will look out for you. People are quicker to give you those opportunities when you prove yourself. It becomes a "no brainer."

B.O.S.S.: Should someone who is looking to become a producer/director relocate to make their dreams come true?

Jesse: If that is what they believe needs to happen…specifically, in entertainment I think it's good to relocate. But there are people who are very successful who are not in those big cities. In today's world, with technology, you can almost be anywhere. It depends more on what you can bring to the market. You do need to come to those cities to build relationships, but that's the great thing about entertainment, there is no specific road you have to follow. If you have the passion, drive, ambition and creativity to do it, you can probably live anywhere and make your dreams come true. It can happen. When you are great at something, people are going to find you.

B.O.S.S.: What are some main characteristics that people should have to be successful?

Jesse: The main characteristic is that you have to be someone who DOES what you say you are going to do, no matter how big or how small. It may be one of the hardest things to do, but you have to keep your promise because that is really what you are judged on. A promise can be as simple as returning a phone call at 4pm. If you stick to your word and you do it continuously, you become credible. So when you tell others you need something, they believe you and are willing to help. If you are consistent and a person of your word, even when things don't work out, they just think it didn't work out this time. Being able to build relationships and treating everyone fairly are also main characteristics you need to have. Not just being nice to the person you perceive to have the power, but being nice to everyone, genuinely. If you are not a people person, then it may not work for you, but a PA (production assistant) today, could be the president of the label tomorrow. You just don't know who has the ear of the people in power and what they can say about you when you aren't in the room. Lastly, you have to be able to deal with failure. You have to able to deal with success and you have to be able to deal with failure. You can't let the success make you feel like you are invincible and minimize the failures. Take them, learn from them, embrace them, and then figure out how you can build on them.

B.O.S.S.: What do you want people to know about Jesse Collins?

Jesse: I want them to know that Dez Bryant will retire a Dallas cowboy! (Laughs.) Seriously, I want people to know that all things are possible. You can start off wanting to do one thing and end up successful in something totally different and that's okay. As long as you want something and keep going, all things are possible. If you have a goal and you are striving towards it, whether you accomplish that goal or not, something good is going to happen. You are going to find out where you are supposed to be. Keep going.

B.O.S.S.: What's next for your company, Jesse Collins Entertainment?

BET Hip Hop Awards, which I have been producing for 10 years, is what I am working on right now which airs October 13. We are so excited to have so many fresh faces from the Hip Hop culture to showcase on this stage. After that, is the Soul Train Awards for Centric/ BET in November. This will be our first year producing that show so, we are looking forward to bringing new ideas to that medium. We have an amazing host and some great R&B talent there. Then is the BET Honors in January and I am also producing an original miniseries based on the iconic music group, New Edition. New Edition members Ricky Bell, Michael Bivins, Ronnie DeVoe, Johnny Gill, and Ralph Tresvant have all signed on as co-producers for the film. The three-night miniseries premiers on BET in 2016. This is a passion project for me. I have always felt that New Edition's music is woven into the fabric of our culture. When I brought the idea to BET years ago, I wanted to create a film that would tell the story of how New Edition emerged into one of the most important groups of its generation. I am so grateful that Stephen Hill (BET President)--who is also a mentor of mine—is giving my company the opportunity to produce this and chronicle the lives of these music icons. We start shooting in early 2016. So, as they say "It don't stop."

B.O.S.S.

Cover & Interview Photography: Drexina A. Nelson, Photographer | Styling: Arike Rice
Producer: Staci R. Collins Jackson for The Collins Jackson Agency

Phoenix Rising

More about the founder of the Phoenix Leadership Foundation

"People matter…period"

Committed to living by his personal motto, "Build As We Climb", change agent, thought leader and emerging philanthropist, James M. Bailey has dedicated his life to serving others. In 2015 he founded one of the nation's most innovative private equity firms, Greenwood Archer. Through a "Human Capital" approach, Greenwood Archer re-imagines the way America's most underserved communities leverage assets, establish wealth, strengthen infrastructure and create jobs.

Before Greenwood Archer, James served as Chief Executive Officer for the Atlanta Market of Operation HOPE, a global nonprofit organization focused on economic empowerment. Under his leadership, HOPE's southeastern region grew from a single person operation in 2007, to nineteen offices helping more than 160,000 youth, adults, and families start businesses, buy homes, raise credit scores and increase their financial literacy by 2015. Prior to Operation HOPE, James served as President and CEO of Landmark Global Corporation, a Georgia based Real Estate investment firm managing over $7 million in assets by age 27. James' professional experience also includes sales management posts with Bank of America and Hershey Foods Corporation.

A native Atlantan and die hard Georgia Bulldog, James has a proven track record of accomplishment. In 2012, James was one of eight Americans honored at the White House as a "Champion of Change: Following in the Footsteps of Dr. Martin Luther King, Jr." A recognized leader, James is a member of the Leadership Georgia Class of 2015, Leadership Atlanta Class of 2014, AJC's Project Understanding and the Atlanta Regional Commission's Regional Leadership Institute. James has also served on numerous boards including The Wren's Nest, Verbalyze, Inc., Safe America Foundation, the Metro Atlanta Chamber Board of Advisors and currently serves as Chairman of the Phoenix Leadership Foundation.

A dedicated community servant, James volunteers as a mentor for the Priority Male Initiative, an advisor for Youth Entrepreneurs of Georgia, the Atlanta Public Schools R.E.A.L. Men Read Program, and most notably serves as Scoutmaster of the Mighty Troop 100 located on Atlanta's Westside, soon to be heralded as the largest Boy Scout Troop in the world!

Recognized throughout Atlanta and across the country for his leadership and dedication, James was named to both the Atlanta Business Chronicle and Georgia Trend Magazine's 40 Under 40 "Best and Brightest Leaders of the Future". He is a recipient of the coveted Whitney M. Young National Community Service Medallion, the Dr. Martin Luther King Jr. Drum Major for Service Award and the Morehouse College Alumni Association's Dr. Joseph Draper Service Award. In 2010, he was selected as one of the 10 Most Outstanding Young People of Atlanta, in 2011, James received a Presidential Volunteer Service Award from the Obama Administration and in 2012, James was named a National Young and Powerful Rising Star.

www.phoenixleadership.org

Will you marry me ~

When Love Can't Wait

Allow us to introduce the future of Weddings and the woman who will make it happen! As an entrepreneur, having a lawyer in your corner can be one of the greatest assets to the team of people needed to sustain your business' longevity. How much better would it be if the entrepreneur was already a lawyer? See how JC Banks has taken a law degree and a lifetime commitment and turned it into a business venture that affects people on a global level.

JC. Banks

1. How has your educational background helped you to get to where you are today in business?

Attending law school played a major role in who I now am from a personal and professional standpoint. It normally takes people 3 years to finish law school but it took me 5. I always knew who I was and where I wanted to be, but it took me longer because I had to climb that mountain alone. Discipline was one of the key factors that contributed to my success, and was instrumental in me acquiring a Juris Doctorate degree.

2. What is your business that will change the world?

WebWed is my way of standing outside of the box, supporting marriage equality and the display of love for the whole world to see both domestically and internationally. WebWed provides an avenue for traditional, same-sex and proxy weddings to be legally married live online all over the world.

3. What inspired you to start your business?

My grandmother Lucille Coleman. It wasn't because she lived an extraordinary life or because she was taught to be business savvy, but it was her work ethic. She worked for 40 years, never missed a day of work and had the ability to move 13 of her siblings from Mississippi on her own to ensure that they to were educated and had a better quality of life. I always thought that if she can conquer any obstacle thrown her way and I came from her

> "WEB WED WILL SET PRECEDENCE BY UNTERLIZES THE TWO MOST POWERFUL SOURCES IN THE WORLD, TECHNOLOGY, AND LAW."

lineage, then I was destined to be genetically great as well. (BOSS)

4. In what ways have you become your own success story?

With WebWed, I have pioneered and patented a way to legally wed individuals online for the entire world to view and share in their special moment. Also, my husband and I own and operated the only full service eviction firm in Georgia www.nopaynostayevictions.com. I have earned a reputable business name in the Bahamas, China, and the United States based own my divergent and fastidious approach to business. Basically I win, all the time.

5. Details about your business?

WebWed is headquartered in Nevada with a local office in Atlanta, Georgia. www.webwedmobile.com is where you can explore the most innovative wedding experience. We can also be found on the following social media outlets on:

Twitter and Instagram: @mobileWedWeb

6. What Steps did you take to get to where you are today?

There is a quote that I have tattooed on my arm as a reminder for myself to live by the following words:
"From Attorney to Judge, I will stand on the "no" and tell myself "yes". JC Banks is definitely a beast when I am in my element, I stand among giants and yet they bow because I am JC Banks"

7. What advice do you have for readers who are interested in your field or in pursuing entrepreneurship?

Believe in yourself, know your field and the long and short term effects that it has on your business,
GO HARD OR GO HOME !!!!!

8. What do you see for the future of your business and yourself?:

WebWed will set precedence by utilizing the two most powerful sources in the world technology, and law. I see this way of marriage being integrated with the court systems, I see this being vital to the immigration courts, prison systems, and beyond.

Photography:
Dominic Botts
Botts Photography
Nyema Bennett : Hair/ Make Up
Instagram: Webwed mobile
Facebook: Webwed
Twitter: Webwed

The #1 Educational & Entrepreneurial Resource Magazine for Minority Young Adults

B.O.S.S.
Be your Own Success Story
Magazine of Today's Young Minority Leaders

27

Entrepreneur Issue

Hollywood Producer Jesse Collins
shares his path to becoming a B.O.S.S.

Singer Monica Participates in Atlanta HIV Awareness Event

James "Jay" Bailey and his Phoenix Rising Foundation

Discover Successful Women in the Federal Contracting Space

5 Entrepreneurs to watch in 2016

October/November 2015

BET HIP HOP AWARDS Special Edition

Be your Own Success Story

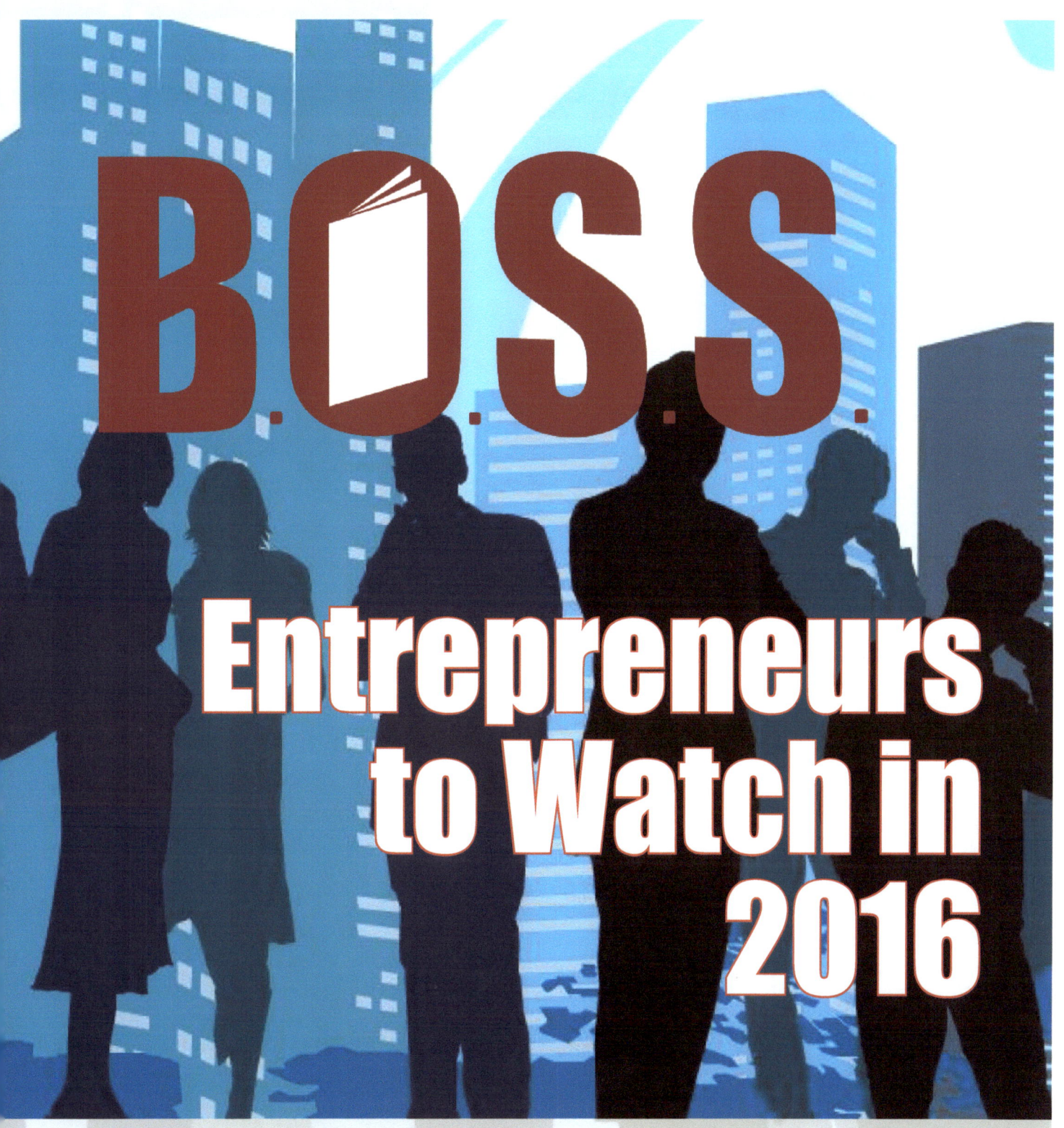

B.O.S.S.
DJ FADELF

Photo credit: Michael W. Eaton Photography.

Be your Own Success Story

The Versatile DJ FADELF,

DJ, Author, Model, Songwriter, Philanthropist, Realtor and Fitness Trainer, has rocked crowds all over the globe from Bahamas, Japan, Paris, Germany, Kuwait, Jamaica, Spain, Kansas, Berlin, Belgium, Switzerland, Brussels, Las Vegas, L.A, Miami, Chicago, Canada, Atlanta, Detroit and hometown New York. Whether it's a huge concert venue, a small lounge, corporate event or Gala, DJ FADELF has mastered it; not just spinning a record but controlling the atmosphere, knowing that there's more to an event than just playing music. He's not just a Dj he's an entertainer.

DJ FADELF, is the official DJ for Three time Grammy Award winning group The Product G&B (known for the hit "Maria Maria" with Carlos Santana and several other gold hits) and a member and an Artist of the HipRokSoul band Guitars N Bandanaz. He has also been the backing DJ for platinum producers The Heatmakerz, HipRock Muzik pop artist Mitsue, Platinum Producer Boola, Ourbit the Label recording artist Shalone and Black Hand Hip-Hop Artist NAT. FADELF is also a songwriter and model, that has had billboards displayed in New York and Munich displaying such work. FADELF is also part owner and lead songwriter for HipRokSoul Music Group. As a member and creator of the A-TEAM DJ'S and A-TEAM LIVE radio show via DTFRADIO.COM, he is one of New York and Atlanta's hottest, buzz worthy, forces to be reckoned with. DJ FADELF, is a member of the FLEET DJs, a contributing mixer to FITRADIO DJs and FUTURE STAR DJs.

Aside from entertaining and inspiring through music; since the release of "Single Man Married Man" one of the most discussed relationship books in 2015, Fadelf and his fellow coauthors have been invited and appeared on numerous, notable media outlets, panels and universities for speaking engagements that surround the building of relationships and family.
Before the release of Single Man Married Man, Fadelf already been in the market of motivational speaking, inspiring, motivating. Giving back is a part of his DNA.

DJ FADELF has been spotlighted in Vibe Magazine, Source Magazine, Essence.com, Signature Hits Magazine, Crossroad Magazine, Sheen Magazine, VocabMagazine.com, Heightmagazine.com and CremeMag.com just to name a few, garnering him guest spots with MTV, VHI'S Love & Hip-Hop Atlanta, Late Night with Carson Daly - NBC, New York Radio Stations HOT 97, and WBLS 107.5 FM. He has also been heard on Party 105.3 FM, DTFRadio.com, PNC Radio.com, Xtreme104 FM.com and other notable websites.

DJ FADELF is masterfully versatile in all genres of music, from Reggae, R&B, Hip-Hop, Top 40's, Calypso / Soca, Kompa, Salsa, Merengue, Bachata, Reggaeton, House/ Club, Dance, Rock, Dub Step, and "Old Skool" Classics. DJ FADELF masters any environment and embodies VERSATILITY!

photo credit: Aric Thompson of Dream Photography

Women Winning In The Federal Government Contracting Space

By: Desha "DrDesha" Elliott
Twitter/Instagram: @DrDesha
www.drdeshawrites.com
Photo credits: Courtesy of B.O.S.S.

The U.S. government is the largest single purchaser of goods and services in the world, awarding approximately $500 billion in contracts every year (sba.gov), with 5% of those contracts specifically set aside for Women Owned Small Businesses (WOSB). In fiscal year 2014, according to the **Small Business Administration** (SBA), 24.99% or $91.7 billion were awarded to small business contractors, resulting in the support of approximately 550,000 total jobs.

How can WOSBs get opportunities to have the U.S. Government as a client? Erin Andrew from the U.S. Small Business Administration Office of Women's Business Ownership sits with B.O.S.S. to educate our readers...

B: What is one reason why more WOSBs are not entering into the federal contracting space?

E: A lot of it has to do with educating themselves on the opportunities available if they do get in the government space, like our access to capital and our counseling programs. Really understanding that there are resources out there that can really help them. I think there are some other challenges, but it's mainly understanding how to get in, and that's why SBA is here. We are here to help folks as they are starting to think about federal contracting space.

B: Are there only certain businesses that will thrive from federal government contracts?

E: The federal government buys everything... they need help with any and everything. The government is one of the biggest employers in the entire country. WOSBs do not have to necessarily find a prime contracting opportunity (prime means that they are the initial business offered and responsible for the contract). The best way to get into federal contracting space is being a subcontractor to begin with, to get your feet wet and to understand what's there. I would also say the federal contracting space, in most instances, are not going to be for businesses that have just started. It's (more likely) going to be for a business who understands their payroll, their billing. You have to understand the payments and when they come in and a lot of the requirements that are there. Getting some experience, looking at state and local governments are a great opportunity, as this is another avenue into the federal government space. There are those (new in business) that g directly to the federal government and that is perfectly fine too.

B: How can subcontractors develop relationships with prime contractors?

Be your Own Success Story

Erin Andrew from the U.S. Small Business Administration Office of Women's Business Ownership

"The federal government buys everything, they need help with anything and everything. the government is one of the biggest employers in the entire country."

E: Events like **ChallengeHer** are a great place to look for prime contractors, as well as matchmaking events. SBA holds a lot of matchmaking events (that pair contractors with each other). It helps identify where the primes will be and you would attend the events where they would be. Looking into industry organizations, clusters, and organizations focused on the supply chain help introduce you to those bigger prime contractors. Within the supply chain you would be looking for your tier-1, tier-2, tier-3 suppliers and they all need each other.

B: Where should WOSB go to learn about federal government contracting?

We have online at SBA.gov, a federal government contracting classroom, which has a lot of online resources for the government contracting space. They can get the ABC's and 101's of federal contracting. Also, go to *SBA.gov/wosb*, where there is a fact sheet and a lot of overview information about women owned businesses and we work with other agencies. Go to your SBA district offices and the SBA resource partners because they are there to help.

B.O.S.S.
J. Pearson

Photo Credit: Alyssa B Trofort

When it's time, it's time. Following years of covering some of the biggest sporting events through a lense, sports fanatic, Jerome Pearson is now procuring and negotiating employment and endorsement opportunities for athletes.

Pearson, Owner of *SportsWire Magazine* **and** *SportsWire Management* **is the latest Women's National Basketball Players Association certified Contract Advisor to step into the arena.** Such a designation provides Pearson the privilege to represent WNBA players and assist them in negotiating WNBA team and overseas contracts and endorsements. It is a designation many people pay a lot of money to acquire, but very few maintain. Representing pro athletes is a cutthroat business. However, Pearson demonstrates that despite the immense competition there is still space for newcomers.

> "It has always been a passion of mine to help people and that's what being a sports agent is all about."

...is ability to acquire two-...me Olympic Gold Medalist ...d WNBA All-Star, Angel ...cCoughtry, as his first pro-...hlete client, proves that to be ...ue.

...caught up with Pearson ...llowing the 2015 WNBA season, ...hich served as his first year ...ince becoming certified in ...hich he attempted to be the ...gent of record for a player ...elected by a WNBA team. He ...ccomplished that goal. Pearson ...urrently co-represents *The Atlanta Dream*'s, Angel McCoughtry, ...long with Sports Agent, Boris ...elchitski, who handles Angel's ...verseas FIBA contracts. He's ...lso the sole agent on Point ...uard, Rateska Brown's, Standard ...epresentation Agreement. ...rown, a former member of the ...emple Owls and Oklahoma ...ity University, was selected ...th woman of the year for the ...merican Athletic Conference ...nd led Oklahoma City ...niversity to a NAIA Division I ...hampionship.

...ess than one year as an agent and ...earson already represents two ...clients. That is something many ...agent hopefuls desire to achieve ...in the first couple of years after ...becoming certified. There is no ...doubt that his inaugural year ...has been one of Jerry McGuire dreams and aspirations. But, let it be known, that he is here.

"It is beyond a blessing to represent Angel and Rateska. They both are incredible athletes and phenomenal women," explained Pearson. "So far, it has not been a walk in the park wearing the hat of a Sports Agent, but I'm enjoying every second of it. It has always been a passion of mine to help people and that's what being a sports agent is all about."

In his first year as a certified agent, Pearson attended 14 of the 17 Atlanta Dream home games. That type of commitment to the team and being around its players went a long way in building a strong relationship with Angel, which greatly assisted Pearson in recruiting Angel as a client. Pearson has been working diligently to arrange WNBA and FIBA tryouts for Rateska and land endorsement deals and a possible reality show for Angel. The *Sports Wire Management* Agent is actively meeting with several producers and networks to assist Angel in getting her reality show off the ground, which will be a platform for the All-Star to tell the world her story. Besides dealing with off-field opportunities, the life of this young agent with a family (wife, toddler, and a newborn) is consumed by finding a balance between work life and family time. These tasks are not generally made aware to the public at large.

"At times I can become consumed in my work, but I always snap back to reality and make sure I find that work-life balance. I always think back to the reason I became a Sports Agent and that reason is to be able to spend more time with my family instead of having a 9 to 5 work schedule.

"Eventually, I plan on becoming a certified NFL agent and I would like to sign at least one player from an HBCU every year," said Pearson. "I also want to continue focusing on women's sports, because that's where it all started for me and it's one of the most challenging and overlooked sports programs. I want to make a difference and help athletes capture their dreams, make a living on and off the court ensuring stability all across the board."

It sounds like Pearson has a set strategy and is executing it quite well.

WRITTEN BY:
Sytonnia Moore